2018年　澳大利亚公开赛
2017年　温布尔登
2017年　澳大利亚公开赛
2012年　温布尔登
2010年　澳大利亚公开赛
2009年　温布尔登
2009年　罗兰・加洛斯
2008年　美国公开赛
2007年　美国公开赛
2007年　温布尔登
2007年　澳大利亚公开赛
2006年　美国公开赛
2006年　温布尔登
2006年　澳大利亚公开赛
2005年　美国公开赛
2005年　温布尔登
2004年　美国公开赛
2004年　温布尔登
2004年　澳大利亚公开赛
2003年　温布尔登

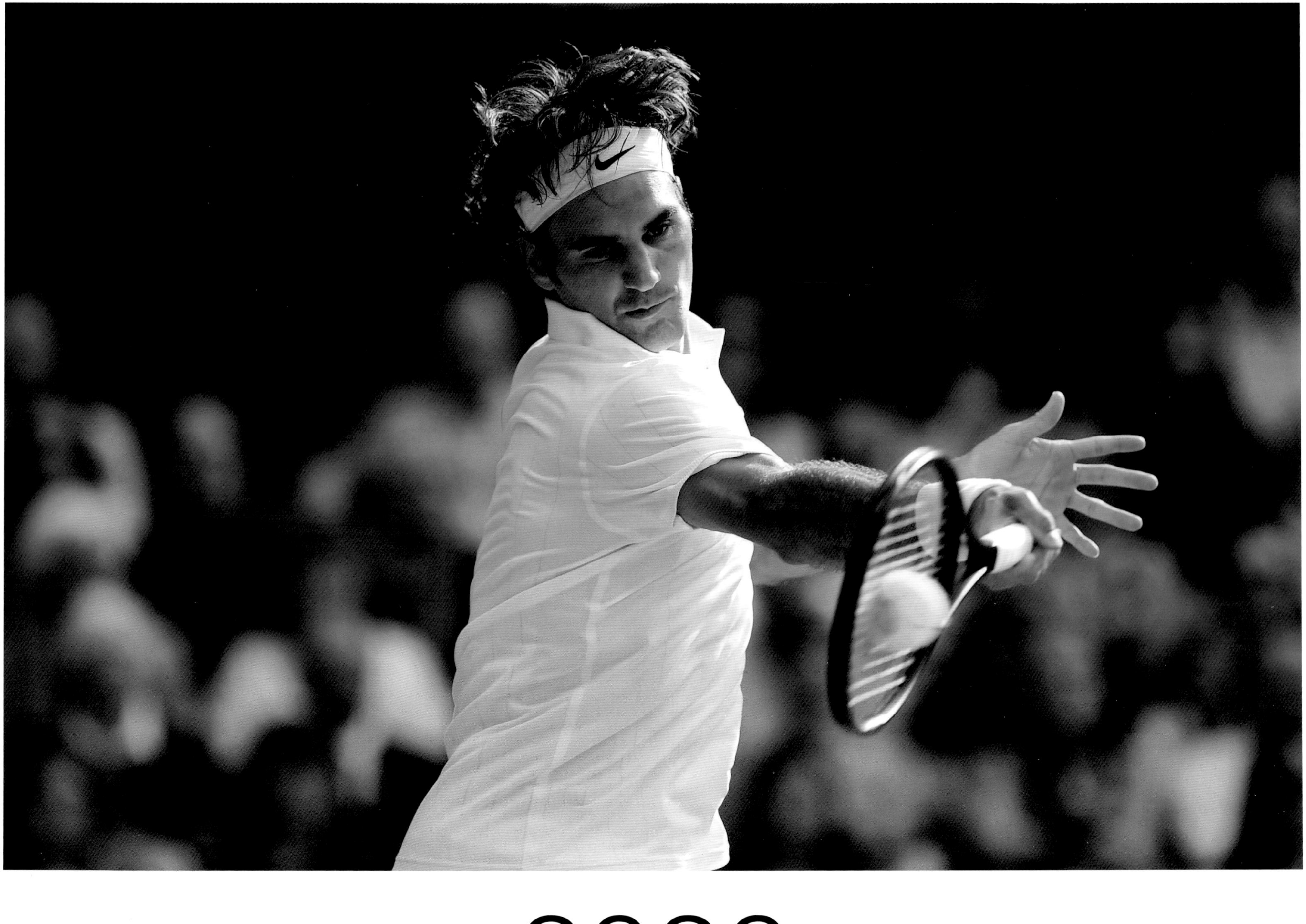

2020

2020

JANUARY 1

S	M	T	W	T	F	S
			1	2	3	4
5	6	7	8	9	10	11
12	13	14	15	16	17	18
19	20	21	22	23	24	25
26	27	28	29	30	31	

FEBRUARY 2

S	M	T	W	T	F	S
						1
2	3	4	5	6	7	8
9	10	11	12	13	14	15
16	17	18	19	20	21	22
23	24	25	26	27	28	29

MARCH 3

S	M	T	W	T	F	S
1	2	3	4	5	6	7
8	9	10	11	12	13	14
15	16	17	18	19	20	21
22	23	24	25	26	27	28
29	30	31				

APRIL 4

S	M	T	W	T	F	S
			1	2	3	4
5	6	7	8	9	10	11
12	13	14	15	16	17	18
19	20	21	22	23	24	25
26	27	28	29	30		

MAY 5

S	M	T	W	T	F	S
					1	2
3	4	5	6	7	8	9
10	11	12	13	14	15	16
17	18	19	20	21	22	23
24/31	25	26	27	28	29	30

JUNE 6

S	M	T	W	T	F	S
	1	2	3	4	5	6
7	8	9	10	11	12	13
14	15	16	17	18	19	20
21	22	23	24	25	26	27
28	29	30				

JULY 7

S	M	T	W	T	F	S
			1	2	3	4
5	6	7	8	9	10	11
12	13	14	15	16	17	18
19	20	21	22	23	24	25
26	27	28	29	30	31	

AUGUST 8

S	M	T	W	T	F	S
						1
2	3	4	5	6	7	8
9	10	11	12	13	14	15
16	17	18	19	20	21	22
23/30	24/31	25	26	27	28	29

SEPTEMBER 9

S	M	T	W	T	F	S
		1	2	3	4	5
6	7	8	9	10	11	12
13	14	15	16	17	18	19
20	21	22	23	24	25	26
27	28	29	30			

OCTOBER 10

S	M	T	W	T	F	S
				1	2	3
4	5	6	7	8	9	10
11	12	13	14	15	16	17
18	19	20	21	22	23	24
25	26	27	28	29	30	31

NOVEMBER 11

S	M	T	W	T	F	S
1	2	3	4	5	6	7
8	9	10	11	12	13	14
15	16	17	18	19	20	21
22	23	24	25	26	27	28
29	30					

DECEMBER 12

S	M	T	W	T	F	S
		1	2	3	4	5
6	7	8	9	10	11	12
13	14	15	16	17	18	19
20	21	22	23	24	25	26
27	28	29	30	31		

Federesque

费德勒式

Emotion. Innovation. Humility. Immortality. Elegance. Perfection

情 怀/创 新/谦 逊/不 朽/优 雅/完 美

马克·霍奇金森——撰文　安东尼·库维切利——摄影
山多尔·萨巴多斯——原版策划　陈超——翻译
上海译文出版社

UNIQLO
Wilson

目录

FOREWORD

Over the last 20 years, Roger Federer has changed how the world sees Switzerland, and also how Switzerland sees itself. Switzerland has long been associated with watches, cheese, chocolates, and luxury goods, as well as with mountains and banks. Thanks to Federer, unquestionably the greatest and the most elegant tennis player of all time, the country is now also known for sporting genius.

It was in 2003 - the same year that Ernesto Bertarelli's Team Alinghi won the America's Cup, giving landlocked Switzerland that trophy for the first time – that Federer first became a Grand Slam champion. Fifteen years later, with his triumph at the 2018 Australian Open, he was still winning majors.

The first coffee-table book about the Swiss, 'Federesque' is a celebration of his unparalleled style, imagination, verve and artistry, with the images from award-winning photographer Antoine Couvercelle beautifully illustrating the poise and grace of his strokes and movement. Accompanying the photographs are mini-essays from leading tennis journalist and author Mark Hodgkinson, who has witnessed most of Federer's career highlights, and has interviewed him several times.

Beyond the Lens is proud that 'Federesque' has been printed in Federer's home country so, like the man himself, is **SWISS MADE.**

Sándor Szabados,
Concept and editor

序言

过去二十年来，罗杰·费德勒改变了世界对瑞士的看法，也改变了瑞士对自己的看法。长久以来，瑞士一直同名表、奶酪、巧克力、奢侈品，以及群山峻岭与各大银行联系在一起。感谢费德勒——这位毫无疑问是有史以来最伟大最优雅的网球运动员，这个国家现在还以盛产运动天才而著称。

那是2003年——在那一年，埃内斯托·贝尔塔雷利的船队"阿灵基队"赢得美洲杯帆船赛，为瑞士这个内陆国家首次献上那座奖杯——费德勒首度成为大满贯冠军。十五年后，2018年，费德勒在澳大利亚公开赛上夺冠，他仍在赢得大满贯。

作为第一本关于这位瑞士人的咖啡桌读物，《费德勒式》是对他无与伦比的风格、想象力、气魄与艺术性的赞誉。本书的相片由获奖摄影师安东尼·库维切利拍摄，美妙地展现了费德勒击球与移动的优雅风姿，并配上数篇简短的散文——出自知名网球记者与作家马克·霍金森的手笔，他见证了费德勒职业生涯中的绝大部分精彩时刻，并多次采访过他。

"镜头之外"出版社为《费德勒式》在费德勒的故乡诞生而自豪，一如他本人："瑞士出品"。

山多尔·萨巴多斯

原版策划与编辑

INTRODUCTION

Watching Roger Federer turns every tennis spectator into an art, theatre or ballet critic: in the face of such artistry and elegance, you find the sport's regular vocabulary is lacking, wholly inadequate. Just as Federer has been reinventing tennis, including playing technicolour shots that the sport had never seen before, so a new word has been required to describe his genius: Federesque.

It's an adjective you might use to discuss a shot, a moment, or perhaps an entire performance – while others play matches, Federer has performances - but it's also so much more than that. You immediately recognise something's Federesque when you see it. When Federer plays an impossibly gorgeous groundstroke, floats just above the court, or bamboozles an opponent with an outrageous piece of skill that makes you wonder whether you're watching a tennis video game, that's Federesque. Quite simply, it's something that Federer can do that no one else can even conceive of, let alone execute.

Federesque can be applied to more than just forehands and backhands; it's also handy when considering what he has accomplished in 20 years of elite tennis. Who else could have dominated the sport in such style? Who else in their mid-thirties could have surged back to the top of the sport, becoming number one again for the first time in years? Which other man has won 20 Grand Slam titles or spent so many weeks as number one? No one else, which is what makes those achievements, and many others, so Federesque.

On top of that, it's also the way he carries himself, on and off the court. In many ways, this tennis immortal, this little boy from Basel who became a sporting and cultural phenomenon, seems so difficult to define, almost a paradox in a headband - so Swiss, yet also a citizen of the world, so poised and classy, yet such an unstoppable force, such a competitor, yet celebrated for his humility and sportsmanship, and at once incredibly emotional and yet seemingly in total control of his feelings. Roger Federer: simply Federesque.

Every tennis champion has some assistance along the way, and Federer is no different. Over the years, Federer has been greatly helped by his physical trainer Pierre Paganini, and by a number of coaches, with his 2017-18 resurgence guided by Severin Luthi and Ivan Ljubicic, but tennis is an individual sport and Federer a singular talent. Those members of his entourage have simply allowed Federer to express his talent, vision and imagination, and to continue to feel such love for the game of tennis.

Spooling back through Federer's tennis life - from his 2018 return to number one, back to his ATP debut in 1998, and then to his first swings of the racket as a boy in Basel - there are words that keep coming up. Emotion. Artistry. Humility. Immortality. Perfection. Elegance. You could distill them into just one: Federesque.

Mark Hodgkinson

前言

当你看着罗杰·费德勒将每一位网球观众变成美术、戏剧或芭蕾舞的批评家时，当你面对如此精妙的技艺与优雅时，你会深感这项运动的常规词汇实在过于贫乏，根本满足不了我们的表达需求。正如费德勒重新定义了网球，打出了前所未见、缤纷多彩的击球，我们也有必要以一个新的词语去形容他的天赋，那就是“费德勒式”。

它可以用于形容某一记击球、某一个时刻或某一场表演——其他选手在比赛，而费德勒是在表演——但远远不止于此。只要你看到一眼，就会立刻认出那是“费德勒式”。当费德勒打出一记精彩得匪夷所思的底线击球，在球场上施展凌波微步，或以一项精妙绝伦的技术将对手耍得团团转时，你会怀疑自己看到的是不是网球电子游戏，那正是“费德勒式”。很简单，那正是费德勒独步天下的秘密，甚至没有人能够想象它，更遑论做到。

“费德勒式”并不只适用于正手与反手击球，它也有助于理解他屹立顶尖网坛二十年来所取得的成就。试问还有谁能以如此华丽的球风统治这项运动？还有谁能在三十有五之时重登网坛巅峰，多年后再度加冕世界第一？还有哪一位男子选手曾赢得二十个大满贯冠军或保持“世界第一”这个头衔的周数纪录？舍他其谁，这正是令那些成就以及许许多多其它成就有着如此鲜明的费德勒式的原因。

除此之外，那也是他在场上场下个人风范的体现。在方方面面，这位网坛的不朽神明，这个已成为体坛乃至文化领域现象级人物的来自巴塞尔的小男孩，似乎很难被加以定义，几乎是一个绑着头巾的悖论——有如此鲜明的瑞士风格，却又是一位世界公民；如此沉稳典雅，却又有着无可阻挡的力量；一位永不服输的竞争者，却又因其谦逊和运动员风范而得到交口称赞；既会真情流露，却又似乎能完全掌控自己的情绪。这就是罗杰·费德勒：纯粹的“费德勒式”。

每一位网球冠军在人生道路上都曾得到助力，费德勒也不例外。这些年来，费德勒得到了体能训练师皮耶尔·帕加尼尼的悉心帮助，在几任教练的教导下，在塞弗林·卢瑟与伊万·柳比西奇的指引下，于2017年至2018年重返巅峰。可网球是一项个人运动，费德勒是独一无二的天才。那些随行人员只是助力，让费德勒展现出自己的天赋、愿景与想象力，并一如既往地感受到对于网球运动的热爱。

回顾费德勒的网球生涯——从2018年重返世界第一，到1998年初登男子职业网坛，再到童年时在巴塞尔初次挥拍——一连串词语接踵而来：情怀。技艺。谦逊。不朽。完美。优雅。你可以将它们合而为一：“费德勒式”。

马克·霍奇金森

Le Nouvelliste
LA MÉTÉO DU JOUR
EN PLAINE 10° 0°
À 1500 M 5° 0°
EDERER DE NOUVEA
NUMÉRO UN
Bila
Süddeutsche Zeitung
NEUESTE NACHRICHTEN AUS POLITIK, KULTUR, WIRTSCHAFT UND SPORT
MÜNCHEN, MONTAG, 29. JANUAR 2018
74. JAHRGANG / 5. WOCHE / NR. 23
La Gazzetta dello Sport
Tutto il rosa della vita
GEOLITE
RICOSTRUISCE IL CALCESTRUZZO NATURALMENTE.
L'ÉQUIPE
lundi 29 janvier 2018 72e année N° 23 198 France métropolitaine
@lequipe
LÉGENDE
TENNIS IN AUSTRALIA
Federer campione infinito
CASTALDO, COCCHI, CRIVELLI PAG. 34-35
L'illustré
www.illustre.ch
«Gagner 20 titres me semblait inimagina
Monday 29 January 2018
Grand slam 20 for Federer
Neue Zürcher Z
Montag, 29. Januar 2018 · Nr. 23 · 239. Jg.
NZZ – GEGRÜ
Le Matin
ROGER Ier
Le roi du tennis retrouve son trône
J.A. 1002 Lausanne / www.letemps.ch
LE TEMPS
Reportage
Au Bangladesh, la détresse des Rohingyas, peuple fantôme dont personne ne veut PAGES 4, 5
«No Billag»
La violente charge de l'UDC contre la SSR PAGES 6, 9
Aux antipodes du possible
LA LIBERTÉ
QUOTIDIEN ROMAND ÉDITÉ À FRIBOURG
LUNDI 29 JANVIER 2018
Tribune de Genève
Federer au 20e ciel

24 heures
Fondatrice du centre Faire l'école en liberté, Mical Vuataz Staquet explore un nouveau modèle scolaire dont la souffrance serait exclue
MPION
incorporating material from the Observer, Le Monde and the Washington Post
DOUBLE ISSUE
APRIL 30 / MAY 7, 2018
TIME
ROGER FEDERER
By Bill Gates
NICOLE KIDMAN
By Naomi Watts
TARANA BURKE
By Gabrielle Union
EMMANUEL MACRON
By Christine Lagarde
RIHANNA
By Adele
PARKLAND STUDENTS
By Barack Obama
THE 100 MOST INFLUENTIAL PEOPLE
time.com
The New York Times
INTERNATIONAL EDITION | MONDAY, JANUARY 29, 2018
Federer prevails at Australian Open
MELBOURNE, AUSTRALIA
A battle with Marin Cilic before picking up his 20th Grand Slam title
BY CHRISTOPHER CLAREY
In the end, amid his traditional tears at Melbourne Park, the most remarkable part of Roger Federer's 20th Grand Slam singles title was that it came as no surprise.
Not even at age 36 in a sport where the spoils have generally been reserved for a much younger crowd.
Federer, like Serena Williams, has redefined the limits. After going nearly five years without a major, he has now won three of the last five Grand Slam tournaments.
TIMES
LUNDI
29 JANVIER 2018
ernational Herald Tribun

情怀

在罗杰·费德勒眼中，这个美丽的网球世界变得模糊不清。他红着眼圈，情难自禁地坐在2018年鹿特丹巡回赛的球员座位上——36岁的他成为最年长的世界第一。就在不到三周前，网坛在费德勒眼中也变得模糊不清，当时他透过“我那一双朦胧的泪眼”，屹立着注视澳大利亚公开赛的观众。

在费德勒赢得墨尔本冠军之后真情流露的时刻，他甚至没看见他的好友罗德·拉沃尔正坐在以他的名字命名的球场内，用手机拍摄照片。在球场内的每个人，以及瑞士和世界各地观看夺冠感言的观众们的眼中，费德勒的真性情一览无遗。

在初登顶尖网坛二十年后——1998年他在阿尔卑斯山地区的格施塔德ATP巡回赛首次亮相——费德勒赢得了第二十个大满贯单打冠军，这是男子选手前无古人的成就。这本身已非常了不起。而更令人惊讶的是费德勒的反应——虽然从2003年首夺温布尔登锦标赛冠军后，曾经有好几回，在赢得大满贯桂冠后他会喜极而泣，但那一次是他最真情流露的时刻。费德勒的儿时偶像波里斯·贝克尔曾说：国际巡回赛场会对身体、精神与心理造成沉重压力，可谓网坛岁月催人老。然而，即使在网坛奋斗了二十年，即使赢下了比历史上任何男子选手都多的大满贯冠军，他仍一如既往地全情投入：“我愿意奋斗。”

费德勒是网坛上既最喜怒不形于色又最情绪化的选手。童年时的费德勒在巴塞尔的老男孩网球俱乐部输掉比赛后会嚎啕大哭。少年时的他是个急性子，动辄发火耍脾气，令到场观看的父母感到不悦。但是，在职业球员生涯的早年，他从瑞士的约翰·麦肯罗演变为巴塞尔的比约·博格：球场上的他镇定自若，在艰难时刻保持几近不可能的冷静，几乎能完全掌控自己的感情。只有偶尔间怒吼的那几声“加油”①（在2018年澳大利亚公开赛决赛历经五盘战胜马林·西里奇时，他就曾吼过几次），才暴露了在平静的表面下熊熊燃烧的真切的渴望、雄心与情感。可一旦比赛结束，费德勒放下球拍，接过奖杯和麦克风时，他就会展现出他有多么热爱打球、竞技和获胜。在那些时刻，费德勒并不想哭泣，但他情难自禁。在年届36岁又173天时，费德勒成为自1968年公开赛时代开始以来赢得大满贯单打冠军第二年长的男子球员，仅次于肯·罗斯威尔，后者在1972年的澳大利亚公开赛上夺冠时已37岁。

无疑，赛前的压力令费德勒痛哭流涕。费德勒之前的所有经历——这是他的第三十场大满贯决赛——并未能令他克服紧张，在整个星期天等候着晚上进行的决赛开始时，那份压力“从内心将我吞噬”。胜利将会为他带来怎样的感受呢？另一方面，失利将会对他的网球世界观造成怎样的影响呢？即使决赛开始后，紧张的情绪也并没有消散；虽说费德勒的纪录令人觉得他是天外来客，其实他终究是一个凡人。

高举他昵称为“诺曼”的诺曼·布鲁克斯挑战奖杯，费德勒赢得了自公开赛时代以来十分之一的大满贯冠军。此外，他成为第四位赢得二十座或以上冠军奖杯的球员，前三位都是女性，分别是玛格利特·考特、施特菲·格拉芙和塞蕾娜·威廉姆斯。他还第六次赢得澳大利亚公开赛冠军，与诺瓦克·德约科维奇共同分享这项公开赛时代的男子纪录②。正如费德勒所说：“童话还在继续。”和最美妙的童话一样，危机感一路上无处不在。它们是欢乐的泪水，它们也是放松的泪水，而这让你意识到他有多么在乎网球。

---

① 原文是瑞士语“chum jetze”。
② 诺瓦克·德约科维奇夺得2019年澳大利亚公开赛冠军，以七冠成就独享“澳网第一人”的荣誉。

EMOTION

This beautiful tennis world was all out of focus for Roger Federer, pink-eyed and emotional while sitting on his chair at the 2018 Rotterdam tournament after becoming, at thirty-six, the oldest ever world number one. Just as tennis had been blurred for Federer less than three weeks earlier, when he had stood looking out at the Australian Open crowd through 'my thick tears'.

In the emotionally raw moments that followed Federer winning the Melbourne title, he couldn't even see that his friend Rod Laver, sitting in the arena that bears his name, was taking pictures with his phone. For everyone inside the stadium, as well as for the millions watching his champion's speech from Switzerland and around the world, a truth about Federer was plain to see.

Twenty years after first sampling elite tennis – with an appearance at the alpine ATP tournament in Gstaad in 1998 – Federer had scored a twentieth Grand Slam singles title, an unprecedented achievement for a man. That, in itself, was remarkable. What made it all the more astounding was Federer's response - while there have been other occasions when he wept after winning a Grand Slam, starting with when he scored his first major at the 2003 Wimbledon Championships, this was the most emotional he had ever been. It was one of Federer's boyhood idols, Boris Becker, who once remarked that competing on the international tour is so physically, mentally and psychologically exacting that tennis years are like dog years. And yet, even after twenty years in tennis, and even after winning more Grand Slams than any man in history, he was still as engaged as ever: 'I like to care.'

At once, Federer is the most unemotional man in tennis, as well as the most emotional. As a child, Federer cried after losing matches at the Old Boys Tennis Club in Basel. As a teenager, he could be a hothead, prone to rages that would upset his watching parents. But, in his early years as a professional, he had morphed from a Swiss John McEnroe to Basel's ownBjörn Borg; poised, impossibly calm in moments of adversity, and in almost total control of his emotions on a tennis court. Only the occasional cry of 'chum jetze', and there were a couple of those during his five-set victory over Marin Cilic in the 2018 Australian Open final, ever gives a mid-match glimpse of the true desire and ambition and emotion that burn beneath that calm. But then, once a match is over, and Federer swaps a racket for a trophy and a microphone, he shows just how he adores playing, competing and winning. In those moments, Federer doesn't want to cry, but he just can't help himself. At the age of 36 years and 173 days, Federer was the second oldest man in the Open era, which began in 1968, to win a Grand Slam singles title, behind only Ken Rosewall, who was 37 when he took the 1972 Australian Open.

No doubt, pre-match tension had made Federer so tearful. All of Federer's previous experience – this was his thirtieth Grand Slam final – hadn't protected him from nerves, which had been 'eating me up from the inside' all Sunday as he waited for the evening final to begin. How would victory make him feel? On the flipside, what would defeat do to his outlook on the tennis world? Even after the final began, the nerves didn't dissipate; if Federer's record would suggest he's extra-terrestrial, he's also very human as well.

Holding the Norman Brookes Challenge Cup, which he affectionately calls 'Norman', Federer had won ten per cent of all the Grand Slams during the Open era. What's more, he had become only the fourth player to gather twenty majors or more, following a trio of women in Margaret Court, Steffi Graf and Serena Williams. He had also won a sixth Australian Open title, putting himself level with Novak Djokovic's men's record for the Open era. As Federer put it, 'the fairytale continues'. Like the best fairytales, there had been a sense of jeopardy along the way. They were tears of joy. But they were also, and this told you how much he cared about tennis, tears of relief.

创新

罗杰·费德勒在二十多岁时重新定义了网球。在此之前，从未有哪一位男子选手赢得如此多的大满贯冠军，也从未有哪一位选手动作如此优美，挥拍如此典雅——如果说网球迎来了自己的君主，那是最稳固与华丽的王朝。有了费德勒之后，网坛不得不重新定义一位球员所能向往的高度。然后，在三十有五时，故事峰回路转——费德勒重新锻造了自己。

对于任何明星运动员而言，推陈出新绝非小事，对于曾经主宰过他的运动并取得真正伟大成就的选手来说更是如此。有谁敢放弃以前如此行之有效的手段呢？而且，这些不是费德勒流于表面的微调。他对自己的技术与对网球的理解作出了深刻改造，这是浴火重生的新费德勒，而效果极尽辉煌。

再一次，就像二十多岁时的他所做的那样，费德勒改变了这项运动。历年来网坛见证了几次成功复出，但没有人能像2017年重回巅峰的费德勒那么令人心潮澎湃：他赢得了五年来第一个大满贯，结束了自2012年温布尔登锦标赛之后的大满贯冠军荒。费德勒令人惊诧地打出了生平最精彩的网球，在他的职业生涯里，他从未展现出比2017年澳大利亚公开赛决赛第五盘更高的竞技水平，在对阵拉法·纳达尔而且盘分1比3落后的情况下竟反败为胜。

换做是以前的费德勒，他或许已经崩盘。但那一年，将踏入36岁的他是崭新的费德勒。重生的费德勒提升最明显的方面是他重铸了单手反拍，从技术到球路都改变了。以前的费德勒频繁使用反手切削，现在他更着重大力击球。虽说费德勒一直是进攻型选手，但如今他的风格更具侵略性。

重生的费德勒依然是费德勒——譬如说，他并没有转变为双反球员——但他的球技得到了升级与提高。过去几年来，种种迹象表明，费德勒变得越来越愿意冒险，还创造了一项新技术——“罗杰偷袭”①：在接近发球区边线进行半截击，然后继续来到网前寻求拦网得分的机会。但“罗杰偷袭”只是偶尔为之，新的反手则在影响每一次的底线拉锯——即使他并未以反手得分，却一直在构成威胁。

费德勒在2017年澳大利亚公开赛的胜利使你重新评估你自以为对这个男人以及这项运动所了解的一切。难道费德勒的黄金时代不是从2004年到2007年吗？难道年届三十中旬的选手不应该像其他运动员那样步入衰退的末年吗？在墨尔本公园举行的这项大满贯赛事是费德勒六个月来参加的第一项单打比赛，之前他放弃了2016年下半赛季的征战，以便从导致职业生涯首次手术的膝伤康复。现在费德勒重回赛场，感受到久违的活力与激情。他带着一个复制奖杯回到瑞士群山，比起之前获得的成就，这场胜利更令他感慨万千。

墨尔本的胜利并非昙花一现：费德勒的复出让他在温布尔登草场赢得几近完美的胜利，在为期半个月的赛程里，他不失一盘夺得第八座冠军杯，这是男子选手史无前例的成就。在即将迈入36岁的几天前，费德勒继2007年澳大利亚公开赛之后，时隔十年再度夺得“完美”大满贯。那也是自费德勒出生以来首度有男子选手不失一盘赢得温布尔登桂冠（上一次是1976年的比约·博格）。2018年初在摩纳哥举办的庆典上，费德勒实至名归地赢得2017年劳伦斯世界最佳男子运动员奖和年度最佳复出奖。在忍受了长达五年之久的艰难岁月之后——在此期间许多人曾公开质疑他是否还应该继续参赛——费德勒仍在高歌猛进。

---

① “罗杰偷袭”的英文全称是Sneak Attack by Roger。

INNOVATION

In his twenties, Roger Federer had reinvented tennis. Never before had a man landed so many Grand Slam titles, and never before had anyone moved so gracefully or swung a racket with such elegance - if tennis had become an autocracy, it was the most poised and refined of regimes. With Federer, tennis had to adjust its ideas of what a player could aspire to. And then, in his mid-thirties – and this was some twist in the narrative - Federer reinvented himself.

For any star athlete, reinvention is no small thing, but that's especially so for someone who has dominated his sport and already accomplished true greatness. Who dares to play around with what has worked so well in the past? What's more, these weren't cosmetic tweaks from Federer. He had made fundamental changes to his game, and the way he approached tennis; this was a new, remodelled Federer, and the effect was spectacular.

Once again, just as he had done in his twenties, Federer transformed the sport. Tennis has seen a few comebacks over the years, but none have been as compelling as the rejuvenation of Federer in 2017, which saw him win his first Grand Slam titles for five years, ending an empty run since the 2012 Wimbledon Championships. Astonishingly, Federer was playing the best tennis of his life; over the course of his career, he had never performed at a higher level than in the fifth set of the 2017 Australian Open final, when coming from 1–3 down against Rafa Nadal.

The old Federer would possibly have faltered at that moment. But this, in the year he would turn thirty-six, was the new Federer. The most significant aspect of Federer's regeneration had been rebooting his single-handed backhand, changing both his technique and the way he thought about the shot. Now Federer, who in the past had often sliced his backhand, was hitting through the ball more. While Federer had always been an attacking player, now he was showing even more of an aggressive edge.

After the reinvention, Federer was still Federer - he hadn't switched to a two-handed backhand, for instance - but his game had been upgraded and enhanced. There had been hints of Federer's increased appetite for risk a couple of years earlier, when he created a new shot, 'Sneak Attack by Roger', which involved hitting a half-volley return close to the service-line and then continuing into net in search of a volley. While the 'SABR' was only occasionally deployed, the new backhand would impact every rally – even if he didn't rip a backhand, the threat was always there.

Federer's victory at the 2017 Australian Open made you reassess everything you thought you knew about the man, and about the sport. Weren't Federer's golden years supposed to have been from 2004–7? And weren't players in their mid-thirties meant to be in terminal decline as athletes? The Grand Slam at Melbourne Park was Federer's first singles tournament of any kind for six months, as he had swerved the second half of the 2016 season to recover from the knee injury that had resulted in the first operation of his career. Now back on the scene, there was a zip and zest to Federer that hadn't been there for a long while. On returning to Switzerland, Federer took a replica of the trophy up into the mountains, and there was a sense that he was enjoying the victory even more than the ones that had come before.

Melbourne wasn't a one-off: Federer's resurgence brought about something close to perfection on the Wimbledon grass where he didn't give up a set all fortnight in winning his eighth title, which was unprecedented for a man. Just days before turning thirty-six, Federer had played a 'perfect' Grand Slam for only the second time, coming ten years after the 2007 Australian Open. It was also the first time in Federer's lifetime that any man had won Wimbledon without dropping a set (the last had been Björn Borg in 1976). At a ceremony in Monaco in early 2018, Federer would deservedly win the 2017 Laureus World Sportsman of the Year and Comeback of the Year awards. How gloriously Federer had moved on from the hard times he had endured for five years, when many had openly wondered whether he should still be playing at all.

THE CHAMPIONSHIPS
WIMBLEDON
IBM
122 mph

5.58
66
44

FedEx

IBM
LONGINES

FÉDÉRATION FRANÇAISE

谦逊

与费德勒在全英俱乐部所做的许多事情一样，这是戏剧性的一幕，但这一次并不是他在温布尔登的荣耀时刻之一，以后会被做成一段精彩集锦，配上激昂的音乐。恰恰相反，那是一反常态的踉跄失足——堪称一部迷你的草地球场灾难片——令中央球场的观众惊呼失色，只有他们会如此动容。

那极具象征意义和悲怆色彩的一刻发生于2016年温布尔登锦标赛费德勒对阵米洛斯·拉奥尼奇的半决赛，当时费德勒脚下一滑，俯面倒卧在草坪上。的确，谁都会偶尔在草坪上失足摔倒，但这一回感觉很不一样：这一回是费德勒，他倒在地上，草叶已经近得碰到了他的嘴巴和鼻子。

费德勒之前在中央球场的所有比赛从未出现过类似情形。在这片草坪上，他曾体验过最美妙的下午，并取得对于一位网球选手来说至高无上的成就。更具戏剧性的是，他的球拍从手中滑落，飞过了球场。他手里空空地倒下了，那是你之前从未见过的费德勒。

2012年的胜利已经令费德勒夺得追平历史纪录的温布尔登7冠，每一年他在中央球场进行比赛，他的动作不禁令人将那与芭蕾舞演员相媲美，而不是与其他运动员作比较。如今却是这一幕。费德勒或许只是在草坪上躺了几秒钟而已，但感觉却比那更久——有人说那简直就像他“力战而死”。当时费德勒即将负于拉奥尼奇，令那一幕蒙上了更加庄严的悲剧色彩。曾经是草地至高主宰的费德勒已经走下神坛。

那个赛季费德勒没有继续参赛，在他缺席期间——他的职业生涯中最漫长的休赛期——很难将那一幕从你的脑海中抹掉：倒卧在中央球场草坪上的瑞士球王。那将会成为他职业生涯末年的写照吗？自从2012年在伦敦夺冠之后，他尝试再夺大满贯的努力尽皆付诸东流，成绩定格在了17冠。

网坛已经习惯了费德勒打进大满贯决赛和高举奖杯。但这是重整旗鼓的时期，对于这项运动如是，或许对于费德勒亦如是（想想安迪·穆雷在2013年温布尔登锦标赛夺冠，成为77年来继弗雷德·佩里之后首位获得男子冠军的英国选手后，英国网坛所掀起的狂热浪潮。而在此期间，有一位瑞士人将七次冠军收归囊中）。费德勒在2016年上半年接受了职业生涯以来的首次手术，之前他在为孩子洗澡时弄伤了膝盖。但自从赢得2012年温布尔登冠军之后，费德勒的网坛生涯并未如他所期盼的那样一帆风顺。在2013年，自2002年以来，他首次未能打进一项大满贯决赛。

即使费德勒聘请了儿时偶像斯蒂芬·埃德伯格担任教练，两人相得甚欢，并勇敢地改用更大拍面的球拍，他还是未能再赢得一个大满贯冠军——2014年在温布尔登，以及2015年在温布尔登与美国公开赛，他都输给了德约科维奇，屈居亚军。在2016年，他未能赢下任何一项冠军，自2000年之后，这种事情从未发生。

在此期间，费德勒率领瑞士在2014年首次获得戴维斯杯冠军，但网球选手只会偶尔客串团体赛事。归根结底，他们是在进行一项个人运动，因为虽然你有众多随行人员陪同旅行参赛，但你总是不得不独自应付各种不利情形。面对自己的挑战，费德勒将再度展现他的天赋，将心情音乐从警报铃声转变为看台上最快乐的声响：一派欢快喜庆的瑞士牛铃声。

HUMILITY

Like much of what Roger Federer does at the All England Club, this felt cinematic, but this time it wasn't one of his glorious Wimbledon moments that might end up on a highlights reel with an uplifting soundtrack. Instead, it was an uncharacteristic misstep - a kind of grass-court disaster movie in miniature – that made Centre Court gasp as only that crowd can.

Heavy on the symbolism, as well as on the pathos, that moment came during Federer's semi-final against Milos Raonic at the 2016 Wimbledon Championships, when on losing his footing he found himself lying face down on the grass. It's true that, once in a while, everyone goes splat on the lawns, but this felt quite different; this was Federer and he was flat out, with his mouth and nose close enough to have been tickled by the blades of grass.

In all of Federer's previous performances on Centre Court, on a lawn where he had experienced some of his finest afternoons, and where he had achieved something close to a higher state of being for a tennis player, there had never been anything quite like this. For added drama, his racket had slid from his hand and across the court; he was down and quite empty-handed, Federer as you had never seen him before.

Victory in 2012 had taken him to a record-equalling seven Wimbledon titles, and each and every year he had played on Centre Court his movement had attracted comparisons with ballerinas rather than with other athletes. Now this. Federer probably only lay there for a few seconds, but it felt like longer – some said it was almost like he was 'playing dead'. And with Federer going on to lose to Raonic, that fall took on a greater significance. Once all-powerful on that lawn, Federer had been brought low by the tennis gods.

Federer wouldn't play again that season, and in his absence - the longest of his professional career - it was hard to shake that image from your head: the Swiss laid out on the Centre Court grass. Was that to become the defining image of his latter years, floored by the challenge of trying to add to his collection of Grand Slams, which had been stuck at 17 titles since that 2012 triumph in London?

Tennis had become accustomed to Federer appearing in Grand Slam finals, and lifting trophies. But this was a period of readjustment, for the sport, and perhaps for Federer as well (consider the British tennis frenzy that Andy Murray unleashed at the 2013 Wimbledon Championships by becoming the first Briton to win the men's tournament since Fred Perry 77 years earlier, in which time one Swiss man had bagged seven titles). Earlier in 2016, Federer had had the first operation of his career, having damaged his knee while running a bath for his children. But, since winning the 2012 Wimbledon title, his tennis life hadn't been as smooth as he might have reasonably hoped. In 2013, he hadn't featured in a Grand Slam final, which was the first time that had happened since 2002.

Even though Federer had some fun hiring a boyhood idol, Stefan Edberg, as his coach, and also took the bold move of switching to a larger racket, he couldn't quite win another major - he finished as the runner-up to Novak Djokovic at the 2014 Wimbledon, and also at the 2015 Wimbledon and US Open. In 2016, he didn't win a title of any kind, which hadn't happened since 2000.

Amidst all this, Federer led Switzerland to a first Davis Cup title in 2014, but tennis players only make rare cameos in a team. Fundamentally, they are playing an individual sport. For all the members of your entourage you have around you on your travels, dealing with adversity is always something you have to do solo. Facing up to its own challenges, Federer would reveal his genius once again, changing the mood-music from alarm-bells to the happiest of sounds from the stands: celebratory Swiss cow-bells.

PROSTAFF SIX.ONE

Adecco
Adecco
Adecco

SECURITAS
EST. 1291
SECURITAS
EST. 1291
SECURITAS
EST. 1291

不朽

那是一个越来越有幽闭恐惧症氛围的阴沉潮湿的巴黎下午，原本它应该是光明之城——罗兰·加洛斯球场的潮润红土粘在他的鞋上，就像阿尔卑斯山的泥土粘在一位登山者的靴子上——在这一天，罗杰·费德勒成为网坛的不朽神明。在理想化版本的费德勒的故事里，天空应该像好莱坞电影里那样一片蔚蓝，而不是那片炮弹般的铅灰色，巴黎人应该带上阳伞而不是雨伞。但费德勒并不在乎下雨；在他作为男子网球运动员取得真正伟大成就的这一天，几乎任何天气他都愿意忍受。

在2009年法网开赛前，费德勒虽然取得了种种成就——13个大满贯头衔令他在光荣榜上仅落后于皮特·桑普拉斯——但他需要在巴黎赢得第一座法网冠军杯才能成为“有史以来最伟大的选手”。只有这样，他才能擦去他的成就纪录中最后一个瑕疵。之前的三年，从2006年到2008年，费德勒在罗兰·加洛斯的决赛中遭遇三连败。再之前的那一年，2005年，他止步于半决赛。每一次他都输给了拉法·纳达尔，后者已经毫无争议地证明了自己是迄今最伟大的红土场球员。事实上，费德勒也是伟大的红土场球员之一，只是他不幸与纳达尔于同一时代在红土场上滑步竞技。但这一次，纳达尔出局了，在第四轮输给了罗宾·索德林，后者与费德勒在决赛会师。

追逐火枪手杯是费德勒网球生涯的一大追求。2003年，费德勒首次赢得温布尔登冠军；2004年，他首次赢得澳大利亚公开赛与美国公开赛冠军；但直到2009年，他仍在巴黎追逐他的荣誉。费德勒如此渴望这个荣誉，只会令这个日子意义更加重大：他直落三盘击败索德林，成为第六位夺得生涯全满贯的球员（之后纳达尔与诺瓦克·德约科维奇也各自完全这一壮举，但你绝不能以为在同一时代有三位男子全满贯球员是稀松平常的事情）。再没有人能以费德勒从未在罗兰·加洛斯获胜而贬低他。观看电视的纳达尔感慨万千——他知道这个冠军对于费德勒来说意义有多么重大——他在沙发上平静地哭了。

更重要的是，费德勒获得了14个大满贯，成就比肩桑普拉斯。在2002年赢得美国公开赛冠军，夺得最后一个大满贯之后，桑普拉斯一度以为自己的纪录将能在网坛保持几代人的时光——甚至可以保持数十年，或许甚至在他有生之年都不会被打破——当然，他没有预料到短短七年之后就会有人追平他的纪录。

春去而夏至，费德勒在继续创造历史。在巴黎取得那场里程碑式的胜利仅仅一个月后，费德勒成为第一位获得15个大满贯冠军的男子选手，那也是他第六座温布尔登奖杯，但对阵安迪·罗迪克的那场比赛却历尽艰辛。那场比赛一共进行了77局，创下温布尔登决赛的纪录，费德勒以16比14的局分拿下第五盘。这场持续了四小时又一刻钟的比赛对于费德勒正在孕中的妻子米尔卡来说一定很不好受，之后几天她将诞下他们的双胞胎女儿。但她的丈夫为比赛划上了句号。

当时费德勒只有27岁。他成为有史以来最成功的男子网球手，同时，也毫无争议地成为“有史以来最伟大的选手”。

IMMORTALITY

It was a darkening, wet and increasingly claustrophobic afternoon in Paris, supposedly the City of Light - and the sodden clay of Roland-Garros was clinging to his shoes like alpine mud on a hiker's boots - when Roger Federer became a tennis immortal. In the idealised version of Federer's story, the skies would have been Hollywood blue rather than the colour of gun-metal, and the Parisians would have brought parasols rather than umbrellas. But Federer didn't care about the falling rain; he would have tolerated almost any weather on the day he achieved true greatness as a male tennis player.

For all the feats that Federer had accomplished before the 2009 Roland-Garros - some 13 majors, putting him second on the leaderboard behind only Pete Sampras - he needed to win a first title in Paris to become the GOAT, or Greatest of All Time. Only then would he rub out the last quibble against his record. The previous three years, from 2006 – 8, Federer had been beaten in the Roland-Garros final. And the year before that, in 2005, he had been stopped in the semi-finals. Every time, he had lost to Rafa Nadal, who has since proved himself, beyond any doubt, to be the greatest ever clay-courter. The truth is, Federer is also among the clay-court greats, it's just that he has had the misfortune to be sliding around in the dirt at the same era as Nadal. This time, though, Nadal was out, after losing in the fourth round to Robin Söderling, who went on to play Federer in the final.

Chasing La Coupe des Mousquetaires, or Musketeers' Cup, had been the quest of Federer's tennis life. Federer's first Wimbledon title had come in 2003, while he took his first Australian Open and US Open crowns in 2004, and here he was in 2009 still searching for glory in Paris. That Federer had wanted this so badly only added to the significance of the day, as he beat Söderling in straight sets to become only the sixth man to achieve the Career Grand Slam (Nadal and Novak Djokovic have since each completed the full set, but don't for a moment think it's normal to have three men in the same generation doing this). No longer could anyone hold it against Federer that he had never won at Roland-Garros. Nadal, watching on television, was so emotional – he knew how much this meant to Federer – that he cried quietly on his sofa.

What's more, Federer had put himself level with Sampras on 14 Grand Slams. On winning the 2002 US Open, which was his last major, Sampras had imagined that his record would stand for several tennis generations - maybe even for decades, perhaps even for his lifetime – and certainly hadn't foreseen that someone would equal him within just seven years.

Spring turned to summer and Federer continued to make history. Just a month after that landmark victory in Paris, Federer became the first man to win 15 Grand Slam titles, with what was his sixth Wimbledon triumph, though it wasn't at all straightforward against Andy Roddick. In a match lasting 77 games, which was a record for a Wimbledon final, Federer took the fifth set 16-14. Over four and a quarter hours, it can't have been easy viewing for Federer's pregnant wife Mirka, who was just days away from giving birth to their twin daughters. But her husband closed it out.

Federer was just 27 years old. He was officially the most successful male tennis player of all time. He was also, without equivocation, the GOAT.

AFFLELOU
AFFLELOU

THE ALL ENGLAND LAWN TENNIS & CROQUET CLUB

完美

当其时，那似乎是完美的网球，或接近任何球员所能臻至的完美。如果说2004年至2007年对于费德勒来说是他个人的黄金时代，那也是网坛的美好时光，对任何敢于想象能以华丽球风赢得冠军的人来说更是如此。和所有的黄金时代一样，那段美好时光终于结束了，但在接下来的十年里，费德勒在二十一世纪头一个十年中期所展现的网球水平仍是任何球员所能期盼的绝对终极巅峰。

我们一度都认为，比起他的网球生涯的其它时刻，那是费德勒最具个人风采的时光，几乎每一场比赛都是“费德勒式”的体现。

但近来这种想法发生了一点小小的修正，因为或许抵达了完美的巅峰后还可以更上一层楼，但只有费德勒才能做到。自从费德勒在2017年重返巅峰并保持至2018年，大家对费德勒的所谓黄金时代作出了重新评估。2017年至2018年火力全开的费德勒究竟能否击败2004年至2007年挥洒自如的费德勒呢？难道费德勒不是升级了自己的网球技艺，将他的最佳水平——以及这项运动——提升到了新的高度吗？这两个问题的答案几乎都是肯定的，但那并不是贬低或否定2004年至2007年的理由。在所有网球运动员中，只有费德勒会令你产生疑问：完美到底是什么样子？或者说：我们如何去判定或评价完美？

就像其他人也在创新打法以保持竞争力一样，比起二十几岁时的他，费德勒的技术无疑更加精湛丰富。但2004年至2007年的完美表现不仅体现于他在最美好的年华所能取得的成就，更在于他能如此长久地表现稳定并收获冠军，在精神上与心理上达至完美。在2004年澳大利亚公开赛决赛获胜后，费德勒首次登顶世界第一，并创纪录地连续保持了237周。这是史无前例，而且在此之前根本不可想象的丰功伟绩。

在那段时间里，温布尔登的中央球场是他展现“费德勒式”的最佳舞台，在这项运动最本真的球场上展现经典技艺，那个老派而典雅的环境与他场上场下的优雅作风相得益彰。温布尔登草场上的费德勒是君临天下的主宰，在2007年，他成为继比约·博格之后公开赛时代仅有的第二位获得全英俱乐部五连冠的男子选手（起始于2003年他在这项赛事上首次夺得大满贯）。

在大西洋彼岸，比起伦敦的夏日花园派对气氛，纽约的美国公开赛有着绝然迥异的球场和活力，但就像在英国草坪上一样，费德勒在这片硬地球场上拥有同样的统治力。从2004年到2008年，费德勒连续五年在法拉盛草地公园未尝一败，成为史上第一位夺得美国公开赛五连冠的男子球员。在他的职业生涯中有各种第一，但这是意义重大的一回：第一位在两项不同的大满贯赛事上夺得五连冠的男子球员。

没有人，哪怕是费德勒，能盼望自己保持赛季不败，但他在2005年几乎做到了，成绩为81胜4负，胜率高达95.3%。或许那就是费德勒的巅峰时期；又或许那是在2006年，当年他的成绩为92胜5负，胜率为94.8%；又或许那是在2004年，他的胜率为92.5%，取得74胜6负的战绩。既然要比较费德勒的不同时代，那么我们可以说从2004年到2006年，每一年都比2017年更加成功，那一年他的赛季胜率为91.2%，战绩为52胜5负。

PERFECTION

At the time, it looked like tennis perfection, or about as close to perfection as any player will ever come. And if 2004-7 was a golden age for Roger Federer personally, it was also a belle époque for tennis, and especially for anyone who dared to imagine that titles could be won through flair and finesse. Eventually, that period came to an end, as all golden ages must, but for the next decade, Federer's tennis in the mid-Noughties remained the high point, the ultimate, the absolute peak, of what a player could aspire to.

More than any other time in his tennis life, we all thought, that was when Federer had been truly Federer, when almost every performance had been, well, Federesque.

A little revisionism has recently crept in, because maybe, but only if you're Federer, you really can improve on perfection. Ever since Federer's 2017 resurgence, which continued into 2018, there has been a reassessment of Federer's supposedly golden years. After all, wouldn't the prime Federer of 2017–18 have beaten the sweet-hitting Federer of 2004–7? Hasn't Federer upgraded his tennis, and taken his A-game – and so also the sport – to new heights? The answer to both those questions is almost certainly yes, but that's no reason to downgrade or diminish 2004–7. Of all the athletes who have ever swung a racket, Federer must be the only who has you asking: what does perfection actually look like? Or: how are we judging or assessing perfection?

There is little dispute that Federer has more to his game than he did in his mid-twenties, just as everyone else has also innovated to stay competitive. But the perfection of 2004–7 wasn't just about what he could achieve on his very best days, but also about the consistency of his performances and results for such a long period; mentally, psychologically, this was touching on perfection. Consider how, after becoming world number one for the first time after reaching the final of the 2004 Australian Open, he held that ranking for 237 consecutive weeks, which was a record. This was greatness on an unprecedented, previously unimaginable scale.

Nowhere during that time was he more Federesque than on Wimbledon's Centre Court, playing his classic game on the sport's original surface, in old-school, elegant surroundings that were in keeping with his classy approach both on and off court. Federer's command of the Wimbledon grass was such that in 2007 he became only the second man in the Open era, the first being Björn Borg, to score five successive titles at the All England Club (the run having started with his first Grand Slam at the 2003 Championships).

On the other side of the Atlantic, New York City's US Open has a very different surface and energy to London's summer garden party, but Federer was just as dominant on the concrete as he was on English lawns. For five years, from 2004–8, Federer was undefeated at Flushing Meadows, as he became the first man in history to take five consecutive US Open titles. Over the course of his career, there have been all sorts of firsts, but this was a significant one: the first man to accumulate five titles in a row at two different majors.

No one, not even Federer, can ever hope to be undefeated all season, but he wasn't far off in 2005 with a winning percentage of 95.3, with 81 victories and four defeats. Perhaps that was Peak Federer, or maybe it was in 2006 when, with 92 victories and only five defeats, his winning percentage was 94.8, or perhaps in 2004 when he won 92.5 per cent of his appearances, with 74 victories and six defeats. Since we're comparing one Federer era against another, he was consistently more successful in each of those years from 2004–6 than he was in 2017 when he achieved a season-long winning percentage of 91.2, with 52 match victories and seven defeats.

usopen.org

perrier
Wilson
orange

IBM

优雅

乏味，他们曾经如是说。甚至无聊、单调、重复。要全面理解罗杰·费德勒如何为网坛万花筒带来新气象——引入了之前所缺乏的精妙、色彩与艺术气息——你必须重温约翰·麦肯罗、波里斯·贝克尔在瑞士人于2003年夺得温布尔登桂冠几天前联名签署的公开信。

在写给国际网球联合会总裁的公开信中，麦肯罗、贝克尔与其他署名者哀叹这项运动已经被枯燥乏味的网球机器人或自动击球机们劫持，这些球员在现代技术加持下，能在底线耗上整整一天。他们写道：问题的解决方式是缩小球拍的尺寸，这或许可以恢复打法的多样性，激发才华与创新，包括发球上网打法的复兴。网球的一切关键尽在于把握时机，而这封信肯定可以位列网球史上时机把握最糟糕的干预事件。仅仅数日后，费德勒在决赛中击败马克·菲利普西斯，成为温布尔登冠军。无论对于他个人还是对于瑞士来说，这个突破性的胜利都具有重大意义——他是该国首位男子大满贯单打冠军——而意义更为深远的是，它标志着优雅重回网坛。

不仅如此，这份优雅是崭新而鲜活的，是只有费德勒才能缔造的现代与古典的完美结合。当某人首次赢得大满贯时，网坛总是会议论纷纷，但这一次情况不同，议论比以往更加热烈高亢，即使当时没有人能预料到费德勒将赢得20个大满贯并成为有史以来最伟大的网球运动员。那天在温布尔登中央球场上，大家清楚地看到，无论21岁的费德勒在这项运动中还将取得怎样的成就（他应该还会夺得更多大满贯冠军），他都将以网坛前所未见的球风去实现。在费德勒赢下他的首个温布尔登冠军之前，有时候你会听到某些从前的冠军和名宿说：网球再也不像木拍时代那么赏心悦目了。然后，随着费德勒成为大满贯冠军，再没有人敢说出那番话。

有一段时间，甚至长达数年之久，每个人都知道费德勒球风华丽。他们质疑的是这种打法能否赢得大满贯。在2003年温布尔登锦标赛前，他从未突破大满贯四分之一决赛。在2001年温布尔登锦标赛第四轮击败皮特·桑普拉斯跻身八强之后的两年里，他还未曾在欧洲的大满贯赛场上赢得一场胜利；2002年在罗兰·加洛斯与温布尔登均首轮告负；2003年在罗兰·加洛斯再度首轮出局。但那一届温布尔登是费德勒的腾飞时刻——他甚至在赛事中途克服背痛渡过难关——赢得首个大满贯将他心中对自身能力的疑惑一扫而空（另一个奖品是在格施塔德巡回赛上获赠一头奶牛）。

观众们更开心的是，显然，费德勒不会去打乏味、无聊、单调或重复的网球，他的胜利是对那些联名信署名者的响亮驳斥（虽然他和他们并没有嫌隙——甚至可以说，他的表现是受到他们的抱怨的激励）。他在场上的几乎一举一动，甚至包括他将一个备用网球轻轻弹开的动作，都带着优雅的气质。贝克尔在公开信上署名时，或许根本无法想象没过多久自己便会坐在中央球场里，在那个夏天的温布尔登决赛结束后宣称：“未来就从今天开始。”

ELEGANCE

Tedious, they said. Even boring, one-dimensional and repetitive. To fully understand how Roger Federer shook the tennis kaleidoscope – bringing subtlety, colour and artistry where previously they had been lacking – you have to recall the open letter that John McEnroe and Boris Becker signed just days before the Swiss took the 2003 Wimbledon title.

Addressed to the president of the International Tennis Federation, McEnroe, Becker and the other signatories lamented how grey tennis-bots or automatons had hijacked the sport, with modern technology enabling players to bash away from the baseline all day. The solution, they wrote, was to reduce the size of the rackets, which might just restore variety, flair and creativity, including reviving serve-and-volley. Tennis is all about timing, and this must rank as the worst-timed intervention in the history of the sport. Just days later, Federer was the Wimbledon champion, beating Mark Philippoussis in the final, and while his breakthrough victory was momentous for him personally and also for Switzerland – he was the country's first male Grand Slam singles champion – it had the wider significance of a return to elegance.

No, you can go further than that; this was a new, fresh elegance, with a blend of modernity and classicism that only he could land. There is always lots of chatter across tennis when someone wins a first Grand Slam, but this was different and much louder and more excitable than usual, even if no one was predicting then that Federer would win 20 majors and go on to become the greatest tennis player of any era. This much was clear that day on Wimbledon's Centre Court – whatever the 21-year-old Federer went on to accomplish in the sport, and it looked as though more majors would be coming his way, he would be doing so with a style that tennis hadn't seen before. Before Federer won his first Wimbledon title, you sometimes heard former champions, and others too, suggesting that tennis would never be as easy on the eye as it was in the days of wooden rackets. Then Federer became a Grand Slam champion, and no one ever dared say that again.

For some time, years even, everyone had known that Federer's tennis was pretty. What had been in doubt was whether it could win majors. Before the 2003 Wimbledon Championships, he had never previously gone beyond the quarter-finals of a Grand Slam. And in the two years between reaching the last eight of the 2001 Championships, where he had beaten Pete Sampras in the fourth round, he hadn't won a match at a major in Europe, with first-round defeats at the 2002 Roland-Garros and Wimbledon, and at the opening stage of 2003 Roland-Garros. But then Wimbledon was Federer's time – he even survived back pain midway through the tournament – and winning that first Grand Slam removed the doubt from his own mind about his abilities (another of his rewards was receiving a cow from the Gstaad tournament).

Even better for the galleries, it was apparent that Federer was simply incapable of playing tedious, boring, one-dimensional or repetitive tennis, with his victory a wonderful rebuff to the letter-writers (not that he had any animus with them, or even that his performance was motivated by their complaints). Almost everything he did on court, even down to the way he flicked a spare ball away, had a touch of elegance to it. When putting his name to that letter, Becker probably hadn't imagined that, so soon afterwards, he would be sitting inside Centre Court at the conclusion of that summer's Wimbledon final and declaring: 'The future has come today.'

KIA
ANZ
KIA
ANZ

HIGHLAND
SPRING
HIGHLAND
SPRING

瑞士出品

对于罗杰·费德勒而言，有一项赛事结束后的派对要比温布尔登的冠军晚宴更具吸引力，要比那个夏日傍晚穿着燕尾服到伦敦某家酒店赴宴更有意义。费德勒在巴塞尔的圣雅各布球场举办的后台披萨派对——在这项ATP巡回赛结束后，他亲手为球童递上一块块披萨——已经成为这项网球赛事的传统之一。（当你吃到意大利辣香肠披萨时，还有谁会在意华服美食呢？）

如果费德勒打入2018年的巴塞尔决赛——在2017年他已第11次打进决赛①并赢得第八座冠军奖杯②——他将化身为披萨外卖小哥，为之前帮他捡球、递饮料和毛巾的球童端上玛格丽塔披萨和意大利辣香肠披萨。费德勒举办这么一场派对，令你对他有了许多进一步的了解。其中之一是他对球童们的服务抱以尊重与感激——部分原因在于他自己曾经是这项运动的球童，那时候他每天从家里骑单车去赛场——另一部分原因在于这项赛事是激发他成为网坛巨星的助力之一。

费德勒被视为一位世界公民——在每一个国家和城市他都受到人们的喜爱，无论他去到哪里都轻松自若——但他仍保持着浓烈的瑞士色彩，跃居手表、奶酪和巧克力之上，成为瑞士最出名的标志。虽然在他之前没有瑞士男子选手曾获得大满贯单打冠军，但他的家乡城市巴塞尔与瑞士全境有深厚的网球文化。玛蒂娜·辛吉斯是第一位获得大满贯单打冠军的瑞士选手，影响了费德勒的成长；更巧的是，费德勒曾为她当过球童。而那项男子职业网球巡回赛离家如此之近——骑着单车就能到达——令他知道自己可能取得怎样的成就。

费德勒的父母都打网球，小罗杰三岁时第一次握拍，他进步神速，一年后就能长时间地来回拉球。怀着成为未来网球之星的梦想，费德勒在老男孩网球俱乐部受训、参赛和成长，遇到彼得·卡特，每时每刻都在对着家里的橱柜和车库门打球练习。14岁时，费德勒自己作出决定，要到埃居布朗的瑞士国家网球中心受训；只有这样，他才有最大的机会成就自己。

两年后，16岁的他成为1998年温布尔登锦标赛少年组冠军，从此他的网球事业突飞猛进。不久之后，他初次在ATP赛事亮相，获得格施塔德巡回赛的外卡，首轮输给了当时世界排名88位的阿根廷选手卢卡斯·阿诺德·科尔。但他初登男子职业网坛的那个赛季最具意义的登台亮相是以外卡选手身份出战巴塞尔赛事，首轮输给了安德烈·阿加西。费德勒继续在网坛节节攀升，1999年在布雷斯特首次赢得地位仅次于ATP巡回赛的ATP挑战赛冠军，并在2000年首次打进ATP巴塞尔决赛。2001年在温布尔登锦标赛第四轮他战胜了皮特·桑普拉斯——这是两人的唯一交锋——让他向更加广阔的网球世界展现了自己的天赋。同年他在米兰赢得首座ATP巡回赛冠军杯。

或许，只是或许，某位参加了费德勒赛后派对的球童将登上这项运动的最高舞台。款待球童是举行那些派对的原因之一，同时他也希望能为他们送上鼓励。

---

① 截至2017年，费德勒打入瑞士巴塞尔巡回赛决赛的次数应该是13次，分别是2000年、2001年、2006年、2007年、2008年、2009年、2010年、2011年、2012年、2013年、2014年、2015年及2017年。
② 2018年，罗杰·费德勒在瑞士巴塞尔巡回赛中夺得第九座冠军奖杯。

SWISS MADE

For Roger Federer, there's a post-tournament party that holds even greater appeal than Wimbledon's Champions' Dinner, and which is loaded with more significance than that summer evening wearing a tuxedo to a London hotel. Federer's backstage pizza party at Basel's St. Jakobshalle – where he hands out slices to the ball-kids at the conclusion of the ATP tournament – has become one of the traditions of the tennis tour (who needs a formal dress code, or fine food, when you have pepperoni pizza?).

If Federer reaches the Basel final, and in 2017 he made his 11th appearance at that stage of the tournament, winning his eighth title, he will later morph into a pizza delivery boy, offering the margherita and the pepperoni to the kids who had earlier been fetching tennis balls, drinks bottles and towels for him. That Federer throws that party tells you a couple of things about him. One is the respect and gratitude he has for what the ball-kids do – in part, because he was himself once a ball-boy at the tournament, when he would ride his bike in from his home every day – and the other is how the event helped to motivate him to become the force he is today.

As much as Federer is regarded as a citizen of the world - he's adored in every country and city, and he's at ease wherever he goes - he's very much Swiss Made, moving above watches, cheese and chocolates to become Switzerland's most famous export. While no Swiss man had previously won a Grand Slam singles title, there was a strong tennis culture in his home city, Basel, and across Switzerland. Martina Hingis, who was the first Swiss of either sex to land a singles major, was an influence on him, especially as he also ball-boyed for her. But having that ATP tournament so close to his home - within cycling distance - showed him what was possible.

Both of Federer's parents played tennis, and having first held a racket at the age of three, a young Roger progressed so quickly that within a year he could keep a long rally going. Growing up, Federer trained and competed at the Old Boys Tennis Club, dreamt of future tennis glories, met Peter Carter and spent every moment practising against the kitchen cupboards and garage doors of his family home. At the age of 14, and quite unilaterally, Federer decided he needed to move to Ecublens, to the Swiss National Tennis Centre, if he was to give himself the best possible chance of making something of himself.

Just a couple of years later, at 16, he was the junior Wimbledon champion with his triumph in the 1998 boys' singles tournament, and from there his tennis career accelerated. Within days, he was making his first appearance at an ATP tournament after receiving a wild card into Gstaad, where he lost in the first round to Lucas Arnold Ker, an Argentine then ranked 88th in the world. But the most meaningful of his primetime ATP appearances that season was when he competed in Basel as a wild card, losing to Andre Agassi in the first round. Moving up in the tennis world, Federer won his first title on the ATP Challenger Tour, the tier below the main ATP tour, in Brest in 1999, and in 2000 he made the Basel ATP final for the first time. With his fourth-round victory over Pete Sampras at the 2001 Wimbledon Championships – which would be their only meeting - he announced his talent to the wider tennis world. That was also the year that he won his first ATP title, in Milan.

Perhaps, just perhaps, one of the ball-kids at one of Federer's post-match parties will go on to play the sport at the highest level. Feeding the ball-kids is one reason for those parties; he also wishes to inspire them.

未来

当你展望罗杰·费德勒的未来，并尝试预测一手持拍一手拿球在网坛闯荡的他还将取得什么样的成就时，你应该知道他与时间的关系同其他球员截然不同。比起这项运动的其他选手，费德勒能在一分钟内做到更多事情，在职业生涯中原本应该走下坡路的阶段仍提升着自己的网球水平。正如费德勒的一位赞助商庆祝他在2018年澳大利亚公开赛夺冠时在推特话题标签里所写的："这位瑞士人比时间更强大。"

一分钟拿下发球局是费德勒的专利，将他的天赋浓缩于60秒或更短的时间里，是几近完美的网球。那种节奏正是"费德勒式"，这也是为什么他能取得曾被认为他这个年纪的运动员不可能获得的成就。当他在2018年2月重返世界第一，在36岁成为最年长的世界第一男子选手时，距离他首次登顶已经过去了14个赛季。赢得2017年温布尔登冠军之后，在提到自己对参赛计划作了精简时，费德勒形容自己要当一个业余选手，但这并没有令他在对阵全职参赛的对手时处于劣势。

在2017年和2018年间，有时候我们似乎觉得时间并没有束缚住他的天赋与理想。费德勒已经取得了作为三十过五的选手本不应有的成就，只要他免于伤病困扰，你可以想象他将继续取得许许多多的成就。以前人们认为吉米·康纳斯夺得109个单打冠军是永远不会被打破的纪录之一——事实上，有些人认为无人能够接近这一纪录——但东山再起的费德勒将很有机会超越这个数字。

费德勒的复出一次次让人们猜想这位老而弥坚的选手可能实现的成就。安德烈·阿加西曾经是年过三旬的网球选手的标杆——他在33岁时成为最年长的世界第一选手——然后费德勒出现了。费德勒已经独步男子网坛，拿下最多的大满贯冠军；因此，或许他需要放眼女子网坛——玛格丽特·考特赢得24个大满贯冠军，塞蕾娜·威廉姆斯23个，施特菲·格拉芙22个——作为对自己的挑战，立志成为跨越男女网坛的最成功选手。

无论费德勒的网球生涯末期会有怎样的表现，有一点你可以肯定：他对网球的热爱不会磨灭。多年来，我们见到其他球员的热情被巡回参赛的网球生活逐渐消磨殆尽，但费德勒并非如此。费德勒享受作为网球运动员的每一个方面——参赛、旅行、练习、与媒体和赞助商打交道——这一切都让他感到那么新鲜有趣。现在即将年届四旬，费德勒仍以与孩提时对着橱柜乒乒乓乓打网球时同样的精神、乐趣和热情在竞技参赛。

或许费德勒最伟大的成就，甚至比他所有大满贯和排名世界第一周数更伟大的成就，是他从未失去参与这项运动的乐趣。

"说到底，我仍在参赛的原因是看到我的父母那么骄傲和开心。他们喜欢来现场观战。这令我开心，也发挥得更好。当然，是我的妻子令这一切成为可能。没有她的支持，或许多年前我就不再打网球了。但几年前我们曾经开诚布公地交谈过，讨论她是否乐意这么做。她那么支持我，令我觉得很幸福，她也愿意承担起照顾孩子们的繁重工作。我也一样，因为我不愿意与孩子们分开超过两个星期。如果她表示拒绝，这种生活是无法维持的。"

THE FUTURE

Anyone peering into Roger Federer's future, and trying to predict what more he will accomplish during his adventures with a racket and ball, should know his relationship with time is wholly different to other players'. Federer can squeeze more into a minute than anyone else in the sport, while elevating his tennis at a stage in his career when he should have been in decline. As one of Federer's sponsors put it in a hashtag to celebrate his success at the 2018 Australian Open, the Swiss is #strongerthantime.

One-minute service games are a Federer speciality, with his genius condensed into 60 seconds, or under, of something close to tennis perfection. That pace is Federesque, but then so is how he has been accomplishing what was once considered impossible for a player of his age. When he returned to world number one in February 2018, so becoming at 36 the oldest man to have held that ranking, it was some 14 seasons after he had first had that alpha status. Going part-time, which is how Federer described himself after winning the 2017 Wimbledon title, on account of his lighter schedule, hasn't exactly held him back against his full-time opponents.

There were moments during 2017, and also 2018, when it seemed as though time was no constraint on his talents and ambitions. Already, Federer has achieved things that players in their mid-thirties aren't supposed to and, just so long as he stays free of injuries, you have to imagine he will go on to achieve a great deal more. It used to be thought that Jimmy Connors' collection of 109 singles titles was one of those records that would never be surpassed – indeed, some considered that no one would even come close to that figure – but a resurgent Federer has given himself a real chance of passing that number.

Again and again, Federer's resurgence is making people question what's possible for a player of his vintage. Andre Agassi was meant to have been the gold standard for thirty-something tennis players - he had been 33 when he held the number one ranking, making him the oldest ever man at the top of the standings - and then Federer came along. Federer is already out on his own in the men's game with the most Grand Slams, so perhaps he needs to look to the women's game - to Margaret Court on 24 majors, Serena Williams on 23 and Steffi Graf on 22 - for a challenge, and aspire to become the most successful player of either sex.

However the remainder of Federer's career plays out, you can be sure of this: he won't fall out of love with tennis. Over the years, we have watched as others have been slowly ground down by the travelling tennis life, but Federer hasn't been. Federer enjoys every aspect of being a tennis player – the competition, the travel, the practice, the dealings with media and sponsors – and that helps to keep him fresh and interested. Not far off 40 now, Federer plays with much the same spirit, abandon and enthusiasm that he had as a child when bashing tennis balls against the kitchen cupboards.

Maybe Federer's greatest accomplishment, above even all his Grand Slams, and all those weeks as number one; is that he has never lost any of his joy at playing this game.

"At the end it's seeing that my parents are incredibly proud and happy that I'm still doing it. They enjoy coming to tournaments. That makes me happy and play better. Then, of course, my wife who makes it all possible. Without her support, I wouldn't be playing tennis no more since many years. But we had a very open conversation, if she was happy to do this or not, years ago. I'm happy that she's super supportive, and she's willing to take on a massive workload with the kiddies. Same for me, because I wouldn't want to be away from my kids for more than two weeks. This life wouldn't work if she said no."

UNI QLO

UNI
QLO

UNI
QLO

UNI
QLO

UNI
QLO

IBM
JAGUAR
122 mph

“罗杰·费德勒是我见过的球风最华丽的球员。他无所不能，而且显得如此轻松写意。”

约翰·麦肯罗

留言簿

“今天我打出了自己的最佳水平，作出了种种尝试，但无一奏效。当你发挥出那种竞技水平，可他还是能打出那些精彩击球时，你真的不得不纳闷他到底是否与你来自同一个星球。”

诺瓦克·德约科维奇

“我们在见证历史。他是当今地球上最具统治力的运动员。”

吉姆·库里埃

“罗杰是与我交手过的最出色的球员。与其他人交手——这些年来我与许多球员交过手——总是有安全地带，总是有空当可以回球，总是有某处可以集中火力攻击，总是会有办法的。但与罗杰交手时根本无计可施。他的打法是如此特别，我从前根本没有见过。”

安德烈·阿加西

“我从未与打得那么快的人交过手。他根本没有任何弱点。他确实配得上‘有史以来最佳球员’这个称号。”

罗宾·索德林

“我能像罗杰那样落泪，但遗憾的是，我不能打得像他那么好。”

安迪·穆雷

“如果有人说我打得比罗杰好，那我觉得他对网球根本一无所知。”

拉法·纳达尔

"罗杰·费德勒是罕见的天赋异禀的运动员之一，似乎不受某些物理定律的约束，至少在部分程度上是这样……他从来不会仓皇失措或失去平衡。呼啸而来的球似乎会违背定律为他多停留一刹那。他的移动是如此轻盈灵动，超越了竞技层面……特别是在温布尔登球场上，穿着这项赛事仍规定的一袭白衣白裤，他看上去就像（我心目中）由血肉与光明构成的精灵。"

小说家戴维·福斯特·华莱士

“罗杰·费德勒是唯一一个会让我去观察其击球动作的球员。他的球风实在是赏心悦目。他能打出你能想象的每一个击球。我愿意去观看他练球，他真是太棒了。”

伊万·伦德尔

“罗杰所打出的精彩网球应该被列为禁手。”

特蕾西·奥斯汀

“我们当中出了一个瑞士球员，我此前从未在其他人身上见过他那样的球风——是的，我指的是任何人。能够见到这么一位球员，我们是何其幸运。”

波里斯·贝克尔

“他的移动宛如一声轻语，而杀伤力却如同一部落锤粉碎机。我根本无法解释他是如何做到的。”

尼克·波利泰尼

“我盼望着有那么一天，我能化身为他，去体验那样子打球究竟是怎样的感受。”

马茨·维兰德

"当我看着费德勒时，我是他的粉丝。我欣赏他的球风，钦佩他的为人。无论在场上场下，他都那么有范儿。"

皮特·桑普拉斯

“在一场比赛中，他能凭借着坚韧、斗志和创造力，让自己摆脱极其不利的困境。”

马可·齐乌德内利

"噢，把我与罗杰相提并论是我的光荣。他是无所不能的、难以置信的天才。罗杰也许是有史以来最伟大的网球运动员。"

罗德·拉沃尔

"当罗杰挂拍时，对于我们球迷来说，那将会是一个伤心的日子。"

比尔·盖茨

20/20 – FEDERER'S 20 GRAND SLAMS

2003年温布尔登

2004年澳大利亚公开赛

2004年温布尔登

2004年美国公开赛

2005年温布尔登

2007年温布尔登

2007年美国公开赛

2008年美国公开赛

2009年罗兰・加洛斯

2009年温布尔登

20/20——费德勒的20个大满贯

2005年美国公开赛

2006年澳大利亚公开赛

2006年温布尔登

2006年美国公开赛

2007年澳大利亚公开赛

2010年澳大利亚公开赛

2012年温布尔登

2017年澳大利亚公开赛

2017年温布尔登

2018年澳大利亚公开赛

20年顶尖网坛职业生涯

1998年
比赛胜/负：2/3
奖金：2万6370美元
冠军：0
大满贯冠军：0
大满贯累计总数：0
年终排名：301

1999年
比赛胜/负：13/17
奖金：20万986美元
冠军：0
大满贯冠军：0
大满贯累计总数：0
年终排名：64

2000年
比赛胜/负：36/30
奖金：46万8974美元
冠军：0
大满贯冠军：0
大满贯累计总数：0
年终排名：29

2001年
比赛胜/负：49/21
奖金：77万3591美元
冠军：1
大满贯冠军：0
大满贯累计总数：0
年终排名：13

2002年
比赛胜/负：58/22
奖金：184万美元
冠军：3
大满贯冠军：0
大满贯累计总数：0
年终排名：6

2003年
比赛胜/负：78/17
奖金：388万美元
冠军：7
大满贯冠军：1（温布尔登）
大满贯累计总数：1
年终排名：2

2004年
比赛胜/负：74/6
奖金：634万美元
冠军：11
大满贯冠军：3
（澳大利亚公开赛、温布尔登、美国公开赛）
大满贯累计总数：4
年终排名：1

2005年
比赛胜/负：81/4
奖金：611万美元
冠军：11
大满贯冠军：2（温布尔登、美国公开赛）
大满贯累计总数：6
年终排名：1

2006年
比赛胜/负：92/5
奖金：833万美元
冠军：12
大满贯冠军：3
（澳大利亚公开赛、温布尔登、美国公开赛）
大满贯累计总数：9
年终排名：1

2007年
比赛胜/负：68/9
奖金：1千110万美元
冠军：8
大满贯冠军：3
（澳大利亚公开赛、温布尔登、美国公开赛）
大满贯累计总数：12
年终排名：1

2008年
比赛胜/负：66/15
奖金：588万美元
冠军：4
大满贯冠军：1（美国公开赛）
大满贯累计总数：13
年终排名：2

2009年
比赛胜/负：61/12
奖金：876万美元
冠军：4
大满贯冠军：2（罗兰·加洛斯、温布尔登）
大满贯累计总数：15
年终排名：1

2010年
比赛胜/负：65/13
奖金：769万美元
冠军：5
大满贯冠军：1（澳大利亚公开赛）
大满贯累计总数：16
年终排名：2

2011年
比赛胜/负：64/12
奖金：632万美元
冠军：4
大满贯冠军：0
大满贯累计总数：16
年终排名：3

2012年
比赛胜/负：71/12
奖金：858万美元
冠军：6
大满贯冠军：1（温布尔登）
大满贯累计总数：17
年终排名：2

2013年
比赛胜/负：45/17
奖金：319万美元
冠军：1
大满贯冠军：0
大满贯累计总数：17
年终排名：6

2014年
比赛胜/负：73/12
奖金：934万美元
冠军：5
大满贯冠军：0
大满贯累计总数：17
年终排名：2

2015年
比赛胜/负：63/11
奖金：868万美元
冠军：6
大满贯冠军：0
大满贯累计总数：17
年终排名：3

2016年
比赛胜/负：21/7
奖金：153万美元
冠军：0
大满贯冠军：0
大满贯累计总数：17
年终排名：16

2017年
比赛胜/负：52/5
奖金：1 310万美元
冠军：7
大满贯冠军：2（澳大利亚公开赛、温布尔登）
大满贯累计总数：19
年终排名：2

2018年
比赛胜/负：48/10
奖金：862万美元
冠军：4
大满贯冠军：1（澳大利亚公开赛）
大满贯累计总数：20
年终排名：3

2月份：鹿特丹公开赛（97冠）
6月份：斯图加特公开赛（98冠）
10月份：巴塞尔公开赛（99冠）

2019年3月：迪拜公开赛（100冠）①

① 费德勒的99冠与100冠是在本书初版后获得的。

历届大满贯得主©

年份	澳大利亚公开赛	罗兰·加洛斯	温布尔登	美国公开赛
2018年	**罗杰·费德勒**	拉法·纳达尔	诺瓦克·德约科维奇	诺瓦克·德约科维奇
2017年	**罗杰·费德勒**	拉法·纳达尔	**罗杰·费德勒**	拉法·纳达尔
2016年	诺瓦克·德约科维奇	诺瓦克·德约科维奇	安迪·穆雷	斯坦·瓦林卡
2015年	诺瓦克·德约科维奇	斯坦·瓦林卡	诺瓦克·德约科维奇对**罗杰·费德勒**	诺瓦克·德约科维奇对**罗杰·费德勒**
2014年	斯坦·瓦林卡	拉法·纳达尔	诺瓦克·德约科维奇对**罗杰·费德勒**	马林·西里奇
2013年	诺瓦克·德约科维奇	拉法·纳达尔	安迪·穆雷	拉法·纳达尔
2012年	诺瓦克·德约科维奇	拉法·纳达尔	**罗杰·费德勒**	安迪·穆雷
2011年	诺瓦克·德约科维奇	拉法·纳达尔对**罗杰·费德勒**	诺瓦克·德约科维奇	诺瓦克·德约科维奇
2010年	**罗杰·费德勒**	拉法·纳达尔	拉法·纳达尔	拉法·纳达尔
2009年	拉法·纳达尔对**罗杰·费德勒**	**罗杰·费德勒**	**罗杰·费德勒**	J. M. 德尔波特罗对**罗杰·费德勒**
2008年	诺瓦克·德约科维奇	拉法·纳达尔对**罗杰·费德勒**	拉法·纳达尔对**罗杰·费德勒**	**罗杰·费德勒**
2007年	**罗杰·费德勒**	拉法·纳达尔对**罗杰·费德勒**	**罗杰·费德勒**	**罗杰·费德勒**
2006年	**罗杰·费德勒**	拉法·纳达尔对**罗杰·费德勒**	**罗杰·费德勒**	**罗杰·费德勒**
2005年	马拉特·萨芬	拉法·纳达尔	**罗杰·费德勒**	**罗杰·费德勒**
2004年	**罗杰·费德勒**	加斯顿·高迪奥	**罗杰·费德勒**	**罗杰·费德勒**
2003年	安德烈·阿加西	胡安·卡洛斯·费雷罗	**罗杰·费德勒**	安迪·罗迪克
2002年	托马斯·约翰森	阿尔伯特·科斯塔	雷顿·休伊特	皮特·桑普拉斯
2001年	安德烈·阿加西	古斯塔沃·库尔滕	戈兰·伊万尼塞维奇	雷顿·休伊特
2000年	安德烈·阿加西	古斯塔沃·库尔滕	皮特·桑普拉斯	马拉特·萨芬
1999年	叶甫盖尼·卡费尔尼科夫	安德烈·阿加西	皮特·桑普拉斯	安德烈·阿加西
1998年	彼得·科达	卡洛斯·莫亚	皮特·桑普拉斯	帕特里克·拉夫特
1997年	皮特·桑普拉斯	古斯塔沃·库尔滕	皮特·桑普拉斯	帕特里克·拉夫特
1996年	波里斯·贝克尔	叶甫盖尼·卡费尔尼科夫	理查德·克拉吉塞克	皮特·桑普拉斯
1995年	安德烈·阿加西	托马斯·穆斯特	皮特·桑普拉斯	皮特·桑普拉斯
1994年	皮特·桑普拉斯	塞尔希·布鲁格拉	皮特·桑普拉斯	安德烈·阿加西
1993年	吉姆·库里埃	塞尔希·布鲁格拉	皮特·桑普拉斯	皮特·桑普拉斯
1992年	吉姆·库里埃	吉姆·库里埃	安德烈·阿加西	斯蒂芬·埃德伯格
1991年	波里斯·贝克尔	吉姆·库里埃	迈克尔·斯蒂希	斯蒂芬·埃德伯格

© 维基百科/男子单打大满贯冠军名录

年份	澳大利亚公开赛	罗兰·加洛斯	温布尔登	美国公开赛
1990年	伊万·伦德尔	安德雷斯·戈麦斯	斯蒂芬·埃德伯格	皮特·桑普拉斯
1989年	伊万·伦德尔	张德培	波里斯·贝克尔	波里斯·贝克尔
1988年	马茨·维兰德	马茨·维兰德	斯蒂芬·埃德伯格	马茨·维兰德
1987年	斯蒂芬·埃德伯格	伊万·伦德尔	帕特·卡什	伊万·伦德尔
1986年	停办	伊万·伦德尔	波里斯·贝克尔	伊万·伦德尔
1985年	斯蒂芬·埃德伯格	马茨·维兰德	波里斯·贝克尔	伊万·伦德尔
1984年	马茨·维兰德	伊万·伦德尔	约翰·麦肯罗	约翰·麦肯罗
1983年	马茨·维兰德	雅尼克·诺阿	约翰·麦肯罗	吉米·康纳斯
1982年	约翰·克里克	马茨·维兰德	吉米·康纳斯	吉米·康纳斯
1981年	约翰·克里克	比约·博格	约翰·麦肯罗	约翰·麦肯罗
1980年	布莱恩·提切	比约·博格	比约·博格	约翰·麦肯罗
1979年	古勒莫·维拉斯	比约·博格	比约·博格	约翰·麦肯罗
1978年	古勒莫·维拉斯	比约·博格	比约·博格	吉米·康纳斯
1977年	R. 坦纳（1月）—V. 格鲁莱提斯（12月）	古勒莫·维拉斯	比约·博格	古勒莫·维拉斯
1976年	马克·埃德蒙森	阿德里亚诺·潘纳塔	比约·博格	吉米·康纳斯
1975年	约翰·纽康比	比约·博格	阿瑟·阿什	曼努尔·格兰蒂斯
1974年	吉米·康纳斯	比约·博格	吉米·康纳斯	吉米·康纳斯
1973年	约翰·纽康比	伊利耶·纳斯塔斯	简·科蒂斯	约翰·纽康比
1972年	肯·罗斯威尔	安德雷斯·吉米诺	斯坦·史密斯	伊利耶·纳斯塔斯
1971年	肯·罗斯威尔	简·科蒂斯	约翰·纽康比	斯坦·史密斯
1970年	阿瑟·阿什	简·科蒂斯	约翰·纽康比	肯·罗斯威尔
1969年	罗德·拉沃尔	罗德·拉沃尔	罗德·拉沃尔	罗德·拉沃尔
1968年	威廉·鲍瑞	肯·罗斯威尔	罗德·拉沃尔	阿瑟·阿什
1967年	罗伊·埃默森	罗伊·埃默森	约翰·纽康比	约翰·纽康比
1966年	罗伊·埃默森	托尼·罗切	曼努尔·桑塔纳	弗雷德·斯托尔
1965年	罗伊·埃默森	弗雷德·斯托尔	罗伊·埃默森	曼努尔·桑塔纳
1964年	罗伊·埃默森	曼努尔·桑塔纳	罗伊·埃默森	罗伊·埃默森
1963年	罗伊·埃默森	罗伊·埃默森	查克·迈金利	拉法·奥苏纳
1962年	罗德·拉沃尔	罗德·拉沃尔	罗德·拉沃尔	罗德·拉沃尔
1961年	罗伊·埃默森	曼努尔·桑塔纳	罗德·拉沃尔	罗伊·埃默森

年份	澳大利亚公开赛	罗兰·加洛斯	温布尔登	美国公开赛
1960年	罗德·拉沃尔	尼古拉·皮特兰吉	尼尔·弗雷泽	尼尔·弗雷泽
1959年	亚历克斯·奥尔梅多	尼古拉·皮特兰吉	亚历克斯·奥尔梅多	尼尔·弗雷泽
1958年	阿斯利·库珀	梅尔文·罗斯	阿斯利·库珀	阿斯利·库珀
1957年	阿斯利·库珀	斯万·戴维森	鲁·胡德	马尔康·安德森
1956年	鲁·胡德	鲁·胡德	鲁·胡德	肯·罗斯威尔
1955年	肯·罗斯威尔	托尼·特拉伯特	托尼·特拉伯特	托尼·特拉伯特
1954年	梅尔文·罗斯	托尼·特拉伯特	雅洛斯拉夫·德罗伯尼	维克·赛萨斯
1953年	肯·罗斯威尔	肯·罗斯威尔	维克·赛萨斯	托尼·特拉伯特
1952年	肯·麦克格雷格	雅洛斯拉夫·德罗伯尼	弗兰克·瑟奇曼	弗兰克·瑟奇曼
1951年	理查德·萨维特	雅洛斯拉夫·德罗伯尼	理查德·萨维特	弗兰克·瑟奇曼
1950年	弗兰克·瑟奇曼	巴奇·帕蒂	巴奇·帕蒂	阿瑟·拉尔森
1949年	弗兰克·瑟奇曼	弗兰克·帕克	泰德·施罗德	潘乔·冈萨雷斯
1948年	阿德里安·奎斯特	弗兰克·帕克	鲍勃·法尔肯伯格	潘乔·冈萨雷斯
1947年	丁尼·佩尔斯	约瑟夫·阿斯伯特	杰克·克雷默	杰克·克雷默
1946年	约翰·布罗姆维奇	马塞尔·伯纳德	伊凡·佩特拉	杰克·克雷默
1940年	阿德里安·奎斯特	停办	停办	唐·麦克尼尔
1939年	约翰·布罗姆维奇	唐·麦克尼尔	波比·里格斯	波比·里格斯
1938年	唐·布吉	唐·布吉	唐·布吉	唐·布吉
1937年	维维安·麦克格拉斯	亨纳·亨克尔	唐·布吉	唐·布吉
1936年	阿德里安·奎斯特	古特弗雷德·冯·克拉默	弗雷德·佩里	弗雷德·佩里
1935年	杰克·克罗福德	弗雷德·佩里	弗雷德·佩里	威尔莫·艾利森
1934年	弗雷德·佩里	古特弗雷德·冯·克拉默	弗雷德·佩里	弗雷德·佩里
1933年	杰克·克罗福德	杰克·克罗福德	杰克·克罗福德	弗雷德·佩里
1932年	杰克·克罗福德	亨利·克切特	艾尔斯沃·维尼斯	艾尔斯沃·维尼斯
1931年	杰克·克罗福德	让·博洛特拉	西德尼·伍德	艾尔斯沃·维尼斯
1930年	埃德加·穆恩	亨利·克切特	比尔·蒂尔登	约翰·杜伊格

创作团队

马克·霍奇金森是网球记者与作家，他见证了罗杰·费德勒绝大部分最美妙的时刻，还曾在世界各地采访过这位瑞士人，包括墨尔本、巴黎、伦敦和迈阿密。他的作品包括安迪·穆勒、伊万·伦德尔的传记，以及《费德勒图文传记》。他曾为《潇洒》、ATP、WTA、温布尔登、ESPN和《每日电讯报》撰稿。本书并未得到费德勒的代言。作者对费德勒在他辉煌的职业生涯中多次同意接受采访表示感谢。

Mark Hodgkinson is a tennis author and journalist who has witnessed most of Roger Federer's greatest moments, and who has interviewed the Swiss across the tennis map, including in Melbourne, Paris, London and Miami. His books include biographies of Andy Murray and Ivan Lendl as well as "Fedegraphica". He has written for GQ, the ATP, the WTA, Wimbledon, ESPN and The Daily Telegraph. This book is not endorsed by Federer. The author is grateful for the many interviews that Federer has given him during the course of his remarkable playing career.

安东尼·库维切利为《网球杂志》担任首席摄影师长达17年。他的第一个拍摄任务是1999年的布雷斯特巡回赛，获胜者是一位名叫罗杰·费德勒的球员。他曾为四大满贯以及全球的重大赛事拍摄相片。现在他成为了自由摄影师，延续对网球的热情。他是国际网球摄影师协会的成员，2013年该协会投票推选他为年度摄影师。

Antoine Couvercelle was the chief photographer for Tennis Magazine for 17 years. His first assignment was a tournament in Brest in 1999 where the winner was a certain Roger Federer. He has covered all the Grand Slams, as well as other key tournaments all over the world, and today he continues his passion for tennis as a freelance photographer. He is a member of the International Tennis Photographers Association, who voted him photographer of the year in 2013.

山多尔·萨巴多斯是本书的原版策划与编辑，是11届乒乓球世界冠军米克洛斯·萨巴多斯之子。上面的照片拍摄于1980年（比罗杰·费德勒出生还早了一年！），是山多尔与弗雷德·佩里爵士的合影，后者手持1929年他在布达佩斯世界乒乓球锦标赛上击败米克洛斯·萨巴多斯获得的奖杯。赛后弗雷德告诉米克洛斯他将退出乒乓球坛并专注于网球，在此之后，他将夺得八个大满贯。

Sándor Szabados, concept and editor, is the son of Miklos Szabados, the 11-time table tennis world champion. The above photo, taken in 1980 (a year before Roger Federer was born!), shows Sándor with **Sir Fred Perry**, who is holding the trophy that he won after himself becoming the world champion at table tennis by beating Miklos Szabados in Budapest in 1929. After that match, Fred told Miklos that he intended to retire from table tennis and concentrate on tennis: he would go on to win eight Grand Slams.

致谢辞 - THANKYOU

除了本书其它地方提到的创作团队之外，我希望在此向我的妻子安妮-玛丽、我的几个女儿，以及所有的朋友与商业伙伴致谢，感谢他们的建议与鼓励。我还想要特别感谢我的密友理查德・福登、迪恩与詹纳斯・罗温，他们的特别支持令这本书的出版成为可能。另外，我要向我的行政助理尼基・萨德维尔与我的图像设计师塔尼娅・罗德里格兹致谢，我特别要提及塔尼娅在挑选相片与排版过程中的奉献、毅力与耐心。

In addition to the team listed elsewhere in the book, I would like to thank my wife Anne-Marie, my daughters, plus all the friends and business associates for their advice and encouragement. Also a special thanks to my close friends Richard Foden, Dean and Jannath Rowan for their very special support in making this publication possible. And an extra note of thanks to my executive assistant Nicki Shadwell and to my graphic designer, Tania Rodriguez, who deserves a special mention for her devotion, persistence and patience during the photo selection and page layout process.

安布罗瑟蒂	尼克	创意导师	兰伯特	多米尼克	友情顾问
布维斯	迪肯	友情顾问	劳	安德鲁	友情顾问
布拉切	玛丽-爱丽丝	天使般的导师	利斯	玛丽莲	友情顾问
库维切利	让	友情顾问	洛利	鲍勃与帕蒂	友情顾问
多明戈兹	乔安	摄影师	马丁	鲍勃	网球摄影师
达德利	基斯	个人导师	门罗	尼尔与凯蒂	友情顾问
福登	理查德	主要导师	皮姆	约翰	友情顾问
格勒斯塔德	拉斯	友情顾问	里斯	格雷斯	友情顾问
吉诺维斯	法米利	家庭顾问	罗温	迪恩与詹纳斯	家庭导师
格林哈尔	阿伦	友情顾问	桑特尔	弗雷德里克	友情顾问
格林哈尔	罗宾	友情顾问	萨德维尔	法米利	友情顾问
吉乌比洛	雷	网球摄影师	史密斯	迪克	友情顾问
亨德森	汤姆	友情顾问	斯托尔	洛伦佐	友情顾问
英奇博尔德	亚历克斯	友情导师	沃尔	法米利	友情顾问
库利菲	托尼与马丁	家庭导师	齐默	保罗	网球摄影师

编者按语

2017年11月，我开始寻找一本关于罗杰・费德勒的优雅读物作为圣诞礼物。经过连日的网上搜索，我找到了30本关于罗杰的网球技术的读物，但没有一本是关于这个男人本身的优雅咖啡桌读物。我真正在寻找的是一本高端图册，类似于我在2012年出版的《莱芒湖冰暴》。因此，作为一位摄影师、出版人与费德勒的粉丝，我决定创造出我在寻找的那本书。与摄影师安东尼・库维切利与作家马克・霍奇金森共事，是一场爱的辛劳。

In November 2017, I started looking for an elegant book on Roger Federer to give as a Christmas present. Following days of research online, I found 30 books on Roger's tennis, but not one elegant coffee-table book on the man himself. What I had really been searching for was a high-end photographic book, similar to 'Léman Arctique-Ice Storm', which I published in 2012. So, being a photographer, publisher and Federer fan, I decided to create the book that I was seeking. It was a labour of love working with the photographer Antoine Couvercelle and the author Mark Hodgkinson.

罗杰・费德勒基金会

2018年初重回世界第一不久之后，罗杰・费德勒在硅谷进行了一场表演赛，比尔・盖茨也参加了此次盛会。表演赛起名为“为非洲而战之五”——因为这次是该系列表演赛的第五场——目的是为“罗杰・费德勒基金会”筹集资金以支持非洲与瑞士的教育项目。
基金会的目标是在2018年支持一百万儿童，让他们接受高水平的教育。“我相信人的力量，”费德勒写道，“他们需要的或许只是最开始时的助力。我们知道良好的教育可以赋能孩子们，让他们将未来掌握在自己手中，并发挥积极的作用。”
www.rogerfedererfoundation.org/en

Soon after returning to number one in early 2018, Roger Federer played an exhibition event in Silicon Valley featuring, among others, Bill Gates. Called Match for Africa 5 - as this was the fifth in the series - the exhibition raised money for the Roger Federer Foundation, which supports education projects in Africa and Switzerland.
The Foundation's aim has been to support one million children by 2018 to receive education of a high standard. 'I believe in the power of people,' Federer writes. 'They might only need some initial empowerment. We know that a good education empowers children by allowing them to take their future into their own hands and play an active part in shaping it.'
www.rogerfedererfoundation.org/en

图书在版编目（CIP）数据

费德勒式 /（英）马克 · 霍奇金森（Mark Hodgkinson）著；
陈超译. — 上海：上海译文出版社，2019.12
书名原文：Federesque
ISBN 978-7-5327-8294-9

Ⅰ.①费… Ⅱ.①马… ②陈… Ⅲ.①费德勒—生平
事迹—摄影集 Ⅳ.①K835.225.47-64

中国版本图书馆CIP数据核字（2019）第263904号

图字：09-2019-760号

费德勒式
［英］马克 · 霍奇金森 著 陈超 译
责任编辑 / 宋金 装帧设计 / 张志全工作室

上海译文出版社有限公司出版、发行
网址：www.yiwen.com.cn
200001 上海福建中路193号
上海雅昌艺术印刷有限公司印刷

开本 635×965 1/8 印张 13 插页 4 字数 38,000
2019年12月第1版 2019年12月第1次印刷
印数：0,001—8,000册

ISBN 978-7-5327-8294-9/I · 5086
定价：128.00元